Kaash: Ek Safar

Regret of Life

KAPIL KATIYAR

ISBN
Paperback 979-8-89906-326-8
Hardcase 979-8-89961-587-0

CONTENTS

PREFACE 👍

Before you begin this journey...
Take a moment of silence.
Close your eyes, take a deep breath, and let
your heart settle.

This isn't just a book – it's a feeling, a
reflection, a mirror to your soul.
As you read each word, don't just understand
it – feel it.
Let it reach the depths of your heart, not just
the corners of your mind.

Because only when you truly feel can real
change begin.
Welcome to *Kaash: Ek Safar*.

Chapter 1

REGRET OF LIFE

I am lying on the pyre.

The wood beneath me is rough, pressing into my skin, its splinters digging deep as if reminding me of every wound I've ever ignored, every pain I've ever endured. The sky above stretches infinitely, painted in hues of orange and red, as if the universe itself is mourning—yet remaining indifferent, as it always has.

The fire waits, patient and merciless.

The flames are not yet upon me, but their heat is already here—curling around my body like a whisper of what is to come. I can hear the crackling of the wood, the hiss of the embers, the quiet murmurs of those standing around, their faces blurred, their voices distant. They are watching, but they are not grieving.

Perhaps they, too, have learned the lesson too late: Time does not stop for regrets.

My breath is shallow. Each inhalation feels uncertain, as if my body itself is unsure whether it is worth the effort anymore. My heart beats, but weakly—as if it knows its rhythm is about to be silenced forever.

But my mind?

My mind is alive.

More alive than it has ever been.

It races, untamed, refusing to go quietly into the night. Memories surge forward, unbidden and unstoppable, like a flood that has been waiting for the dam to break. They come in flashes, sharp and vivid, each one a piece of the life I am leaving behind.

Then, from somewhere deep within my soul, a single word forms.

A whisper at first.

Then a sigh.

And finally, a roar—echoing through every cell in my being.

"Kaash..."

Kaash... If only.

Two small words, but carrying the weight of an entire lifetime.

If only I had lived. Truly lived.

If only I had taken risks instead of waiting for the "right time."

If only I had followed my dreams instead of settling for what was safe.

If only I had loved fully, without fear, without hesitation.

If only I had spoken my truth, instead of biting my tongue to keep others comfortable.

If only... If only...

The regrets pile up, each one heavier than the last. They press against my chest, suffocating me more than the smoke rising from beneath.

The moments I let slip away.

The words I never had the courage to say.

The dreams I buried before they even had a chance to breathe.

I close my eyes, and suddenly, I am no longer here.

I am standing at the crossroads of my life, staring at the choices I could have made—the paths I could have walked.

I see myself as a young adult, standing at the edge of a cliff, terrified to jump.

I see the version of me who stayed silent when my heart screamed to speak.

I see the chances I let go, the people I let slip away, the happiness I never allowed myself to feel.

And now, as I lie here, on the edge of death, the realization crashes over me with the force of a tidal wave:

"Is this it? Is this how my story ends?"

A tear slips down my cheek, unnoticed by anyone except the sky above.

The fire crackles louder, eager to consume me, and yet, my voice trembles with one final plea:

"Kaash... I had one more chance."

But the truth is harsh.

The fire does not care about the life I could have lived. The flames will not pause for my unspoken words. The sky will not stop to grant me more time.

I can feel the heat now, pressing closer, and I realize that I am out of time.

Or am I?

In that moment, something stirs within me.

A spark.

A defiance.

A silent rebellion against the finality of regret.

Because maybe, just maybe... regret doesn't have to be the end of my story.

Maybe it can be the beginning.

Reflection: A Message to the Reader

How many of us are already lying on this metaphorical pyre?

Not dead, but not fully alive either. Trapped in routines, chained by fears, living a life dictated by expectations instead of desire.

How many dreams have we buried, telling ourselves "someday"—only for someday to never come?

How many words have we swallowed, convincing ourselves that silence is safer than truth?

How many roads have we refused to walk, choosing comfort over the unknown, even when the unknown held the possibility of greatness?

And if today was our last day, would our hearts whisper the same word?

Kaash... If only.

But unlike the man on the pyre, we still have time.

The fire has not reached us yet.

The sky is still watching.

The choices are still ours to make.

And so, before another day slips away, before another regret is added to the pile, I ask you:

What will you do with the time you have left?

Because in the end, the only thing worse than failing is never trying at all.

The choice is yours.

The story is still unwritten.

So don't wait until the flames are upon you.

Live now.

Love now.

Speak now.

Chase your *Kaash* before it turns into regret.

Chapter 2

FEAR OF LIFE

"Yeah sab kalpanik hai... isse success ka koi matlab nahi hai... but we have made it our life."

Fear. It's one of the most powerful forces in the world. It keeps us alive, yes—but it also keeps us stuck. Trapped. Unable to break free from the invisible chains we've placed around ourselves.

And for most people, that fear isn't about survival anymore. It's not the fear of wild animals or war. It's the fear of failure, the fear of judgment, the fear of stepping outside the comfortable little bubble we've created for ourselves.

A bubble filled with mid-tier dreams:

✦   A good job.

✦   A decent salary.

✦   A nice car, maybe a house with a loan, and enough money to keep up with society's idea of "high standards."

> ✦ EMIs, gadgets, branded clothes, and fancy vacations that we post on social media for validation.

We tell ourselves that this is success. That this is enough. But deep down, we know the truth. This isn't success. This isn't freedom. This is just survival, dressed up to look like success.

The Comfort Zone Trap

Most people get stuck in what I call the "comfort zone trap." They settle into a job that pays just enough to cover their expenses and keep them comfortable. They start chasing small, mid-level dreams like a car, a flat, and a higher salary—dreams that society tells us are the markers of success.

And then, slowly but surely, they stop dreaming.

Why? Because comfort kills ambition. Once we get comfortable, we stop taking risks. We stop stepping outside our bubble. We stop chasing the big, scary, life-changing dreams that could lead us to real success.

The Fear That Holds Us Back: The Imaginary Chain

We are bound by invisible chains—chains that exist only in our minds.

Have you ever heard the story of the elephant and the chain?

When an elephant is young, it is tied to a post with a strong chain. No matter how hard it tries, it can't break free. Eventually, it gives up. And even when it grows into a massive, powerful adult that could easily break the chain, it doesn't even try—because it believes that it's still helpless.

That's exactly what happens to us in life. We are tied down by invisible chains:

+ The fear of failure.

+ The fear of judgment.

+ The belief that we are "ordinary" and that only "extraordinary" people can achieve greatness.

The Ghost of the Mind (Man Ka Bhoot)

This "man ka bhoot" (the ghost of the mind) keeps us trapped. It whispers in our ears, telling us that we're not good enough, that we can't succeed, that we should stay in our comfort zone.

And one of the biggest challenges we face, especially in India, is the belief that greatness is something reserved for the past.

If someone in history did something extraordinary, we put them on a pedestal. We make them into a god.

+ *"Woh toh Bhagwan ka avatar the."*

◆ *"Hum toh sirf aam aadmi hain. Hum kya kar sakte hain?"*

But here's the truth: You are the only god in your world. Right here, right now. You have the same potential, the same power, the same ability to achieve greatness. The only thing holding you back is the imaginary chain around your mind.

Dream, Visualize, Execute, and Create History

Dream. Always dream. Because dreams are where everything begins.

But dreaming isn't enough. If you don't act on your dreams, they'll just remain wishes, floating in your mind like clouds that never turn into rain.

So dream it. Visualize it. Execute it.

And when you execute your dreams, you don't just create success for yourself—you create history for others. You inspire others to break free from their chains and chase their own dreams.

Because that's what true success is: not just achieving your dreams, but helping others believe that they can achieve theirs too.

Sowing Seeds of Success: The Chinese Bamboo Story

Taking a risk is like sowing seeds in the soil. It takes time, effort, and patience. And one of the best examples of this is the story of the Chinese bamboo tree.

When you plant a Chinese bamboo seed, nothing happens for the first year. Or the second year. Or the third, or even the fourth. No matter how much you water it or care for it, you see no growth at all.

It's easy to feel frustrated, to think that all your effort has been wasted. Many people give up at this stage. But the ones who keep going, who keep watering the seed, who don't lose faith... they are in for something incredible.

Because in the fifth year, something magical happens. The bamboo tree suddenly shoots up, growing **up to 90 feet in just a few weeks!**

All that time, when it seemed like nothing was happening, the bamboo was actually growing underground, developing a strong root system that could support its sudden and rapid growth. Without that foundation, it wouldn't have been able to grow so tall, so fast.

The Lesson of the Bamboo Tree

Life works the same way. Success takes time. You may not see results right away, but that doesn't mean you're failing. It just means you're building your roots—your skills, your resilience, your experience.

And when the time is right, all that hard work, all those risks you took, will pay off in ways you never imagined.

The problem is, most people give up before the bamboo has a chance to grow. They get discouraged when they don't see immediate results and retreat back into their comfort zone.

But the truth is, **real success takes time.** It's not about instant results – it's about perseverance, resilience, and the willingness to keep going, even when the road is tough.

The Illusion of Security

The saddest part is that most people think they're safe in their comfort zone. But that's just an illusion.

+ Jobs can be lost.

+ EMIs can pile up.

+ The "high standards" we're chasing can crumble in an instant.

Real security doesn't come from a salary, a house, or a car. It comes from within. It comes from having the courage to take risks, to follow your dreams, and to build a life that's truly meaningful to you.

Breaking Free

So how do we break free from the comfort zone trap? It starts with a choice.

A choice to stop settling.

A choice to face your fears head-on.

A choice to dream bigger, bolder, and without limits.

Because at the end of the day, life isn't about playing it safe. It's about living fully, fearlessly, and without regret. And every time you take a risk, every time you step outside your comfort zone, you are planting seeds that could one day grow into something incredible.

So keep going. Keep planting. Keep watering your dreams. And one day, when the time is right, you'll grow beyond anything you ever thought possible—just like the Chinese bamboo tree.

Chapter 3

WHAT IS LIFE (JEEVAN KYA HAI?)

"Choti si zindagi... sach mein bahut choti hai."

Have you ever stopped and truly thought about how short life really is?

Most of us live as if we have all the time in the world. We waste days, months, even years holding on to egos, grudges, and petty arguments. We get caught up in the rat race, chasing money, fame, and validation. And we forget to actually **live**.

But life is short. Very short. And when you really understand how short it is, it changes everything. You stop wasting time. You stop chasing things that don't matter. You stop living for others, and you start living for yourself.

The First 20 Years: Unconscious Living

The first 20 years of your life... they pass by almost unconsciously.

You don't even realize it. You're just living day by day, following the path that society has laid out for you. You wake up, go to school, study for exams, play games, hang out with friends, and repeat.

You don't really think about the purpose of life during these years. You're not consciously aware of how precious time is. And before you know it, those 20 years are gone.

It's like sleepwalking through life. You're alive, but you're not really *living*.

And the scariest part? Many people never wake up from this state. They keep sleepwalking through life, wasting years chasing meaningless goals, holding on to grudges, and living according to other people's expectations.

A Moment of Realization

But what if you could wake up? What if you could become conscious of your time—right now, before it's too late?

Because the truth is, **those 20 years are gone.** You can't get them back. But you can change what happens next.

Breaking Down 80 Years: The Shocking Reality

Let's assume you're lucky enough to live for 80 years.

- The **first 20 years** go by unconsciously—spent on studies, games, exams, and figuring things out without really thinking about life's purpose.

- The **last 20 years** also pass unconsciously, with reduced energy, declining health, and mounting liabilities.

That leaves you with a **mid-40-year window** to truly make an impact. But even within those 40 years, how much of that time do you really have to live consciously? Let's break it down:

Mid-40-Year Breakdown

1. **8 Hours of Sleep Every Day**

   - 8 hours per day = **one-third of your day** goes to sleep.

   - That's **20 more years** spent just sleeping!

2. Now you're down to: **40 - 20 = 20 years left.**

3. **2 Hours for Daily Routine Tasks**

   These are basic things like eating, bathing, commuting, and scrolling through your phone.

✦   2 hours a day = **5 more years gone.**

4. Now you're left with: **20 - 5 = 15 years.**

5. **9 Hours a Day for Work (Average Job Life)**

Most people spend about **9 hours a day** working (including commuting).

✦   That's nearly **half the day gone**—and over these 40 years, it adds up to **10-15 years spent working.**

6. Now, you're left with just: **15 - 10 = 5 years.**

The Final Reality: Just 5-10 Years to Truly Live

After accounting for sleep, daily tasks, and work, you're left with only **5 to 10 years out of 80** to truly live your life.

And here's the big question: **Where is the time for ego, competition, comparing yourself to others, or wasting time on gossip and negativity?**

Even in these 5 to 10 years, as you grow older, your energy levels decline, responsibilities pile up, and new liabilities bind you. So, where is the time for life? Where is the time to waste on grudges, egos, and mindless comparisons?

The Formula for Life Calculation

This is not about spirituality; it's simple math.

To understand how much conscious life you have left, here's a simple formula you can use:

- ✦ **L** = Your lifespan (in years).

- ✦ **S** = Hours spent sleeping per day (e.g., 8 hours)

- ✦ **R** = Hours spent on routine tasks per day (e.g., 2 hours)

- ✦ **W** = Hours spent working per day (e.g., 9 hours).

Step 1: Calculate Total Hours Lived

Total hours in your lifespan = **L × 365 × 24**.

Step 2: Calculate Time Spent on Major Activities

- Time spent sleeping: **(L × 365 × S) / 24 years.**

- Time spent on routine tasks: **(L × 365 × R) / 24 years.**

- Time spent working: **(L × 365 × W) / 24 years.**

Step 3: Calculate Conscious Life Years Left

Conscious Life Years Left = **L - (Years spent sleeping + Years spent on routine tasks + Years spent working).**

The Wake-Up Call

When you see life broken down like this, it's a wake-up call. You don't have as much time as you think. You only have a small window—about **5 to 10 years**—to actually follow your dreams, spend time with your loved ones, and do the things that bring you real happiness.

A Bonus Reminder

Use this formula when you feel bored, aimless, or stuck in a loop of ego and negativity.

It's a powerful reminder to wake up, take action, and stop wasting time on things that don't matter.

Because in the end, **your time is the most precious thing you have.**

So, what will you do with the time you have left? Will you keep wasting it, or will you start living consciously and make every moment count?

Chapter 4

RISK (AISI CHEEZ JO HAI HI NAHI)

Have you ever thought about doing something new? Starting your own business? Changing your career? Following your passion?

And as soon as you think about it, your mind immediately starts throwing questions at you:

+ *"Risk lena chahte ho? Pata hai, stable job chhodne ka kya matlab hai?"*

+ *"Tumhari girlfriend ya wife ka kya hoga?"*

+ *"Kaise survive karoge?"*

+ *"Weekend kaise enjoy karoge? Pub, bar, shopping, yeh sab kaise hoga?"*

Your mind starts bombarding you with fears. It makes you worry about imaginary things—about a future that hasn't even happened yet. And because of this fear, you stop. You stay in your comfort zone. You give up on your dreams.

But here's the truth: **Risk actually hai hi nahi.** It exists only in your mind. Let me explain.

Risk vs. Calculated Risk

Risk *tab hota hai jab aap bina soche-samjhe, bina kisi plan ke kuch karte ho.* Let me give you an example:

Imagine you don't know how to swim. You go to a deep river, and without thinking, you jump into the water. That's **real risk**—because you have no skills, no preparation, and no plan.

But let's say you really want to learn how to swim. Instead of jumping straight into the river, you take a more calculated approach. You join a swimming class, practice in a small pool, and slowly build your confidence. After some time, you can swim in deep water without any fear.

That's called **calculated risk.** It's not blind risk – it's smart, planned, and strategic.

Riding a Bike and Calculating Risk

Let's take another example: Imagine you're riding a bike, and you want to overtake another vehicle on the road. You don't just accelerate blindly—you calculate the speed difference, check the gap, and then decide when and how much to accelerate so you can overtake safely.

That's **calculated risk.** You assessed the situation, evaluated your bike's capacity, and made a plan to minimize the risk.

Now, apply the same logic to your life goals. Let's say you want to start your own business. Instead of quitting your job blindly and jumping into the unknown, you can **plan your risk capacity** based on your situation.

Here's how you can take calculated risks:

Plan Your Risk Capacity

1. **Research:**

   If you want to open a startup, start by doing research in your free time. Utilize your weekends wisely. Instead of wasting time at parties or binge-watching shows, dedicate that time to learning about your industry, analyzing market trends, and building your business idea.

2. **Avoid Unhealthy Habits:**

   Reduce unnecessary expenses and avoid unhealthy food, which drains your energy. A healthy body supports a sharp mind.

3. Plan Financially:

Financial planning is key to reducing risk. Break down your expenses and create a financial safety net. For example, if your monthly expenditure is ₹20,000, save at least ₹1,20,000 as a 6-month backup fund. This will give you the confidence to take the leap without constantly worrying about money.

4. Make Healthy Investments:

Don't put all your money into risky ventures. Diversify your investments and build multiple streams of income to support you during uncertain times.

5. Surround Yourself with Ambitious People:

Spend time with people who have higher goals and a growth mindset. When you surround yourself with ambitious, like-minded people, you'll be inspired to aim higher and take calculated risks.

6. Avoid Wasting Time:

Time is your most valuable asset. Don't waste it on gossip, negativity, or meaningless distractions. Every moment you spend improving yourself and working toward your goals brings you closer to success.

When You Start, People Will Judge

Here's another harsh truth:

When you start taking risks, you will face criticism. People will judge you, question you, and even laugh at you if you fail.

When you try something new and fail, people will say, *"Dekha, usne risk liya aur fail ho gaya!"* They will focus only on the result, not the effort, the journey, or the lessons you learned along the way.

But here's what they don't understand: **Risk is not about success or failure. It's about the journey.**

You should enjoy the process of taking risks, not just the outcome.

When you take a calculated risk and follow your dreams, you are already winning—because you are doing what most people are too afraid to do.

Enjoy the Journey, Not Just the Result

Whether you succeed or fail, it doesn't matter. What matters is that you tried, you learned, and you grew as a person.

Success is not guaranteed in life, but growth is. Every risk you take, every failure you face, and every lesson you learn makes you stronger, wiser, and better prepared for the future.

So, stop worrying about what people will say. Stop worrying about success or failure. Start enjoying the process.

Because life is not about reaching a destination – it's about enjoying the journey.

Fear of the Unknown

The biggest reason people don't take risks is the fear of the unknown.

They think: *"Agar fail ho gaya toh kya hoga?"*

And that fear keeps them stuck in their comfort zone. They keep doing the same job, living the same life, and following the same routine—because it feels "safe."

But here's the thing:

✦ **Safety is an illusion.** Even your "stable" job is not 100% secure. Anything can happen at any time.

✦ **Comfort is temporary.** If you never take risks, you'll never grow, and you'll never achieve your full potential.

The Real Definition of Risk

Risk isn't about doing something new. It's about doing something new *without preparation.*

When you calculate your risks, prepare yourself, and take small steps toward your goal, the risk becomes much smaller. It's no longer a blind leap—it's a carefully planned journey.

So, the next time your mind tells you, *"Risk mat lo,"* ask yourself: *Is it really a risk? Or is it just my fear talking?*

Comfort Zone vs. Growth Zone

Most people stay in their comfort zone because it feels safe. But nothing grows in the comfort zone. All the magic happens in the **growth zone**—the place where you take calculated risks, try new things, and push yourself beyond your limits.

Think about it: Every successful person you admire took risks. They didn't stay in their comfort zones. They faced their fears, took calculated risks, and created the life they wanted.

Break the Illusion of Risk

The biggest illusion in life is that taking risks is dangerous.

The truth is, **not taking risks is even more dangerous.**

+ If you don't take risks, you stay stuck in the same place.

+ If you don't take risks, you never discover your true potential.

✦   If you don't take risks, you'll look back one day and say, *"Kaash maine tab risk liya hota."*

Final Thought: Plan, Prepare, and Take the Leap

Remember, risk doesn't mean jumping blindly. It means planning, preparing, and taking small steps toward your goal.

So, if there's something you've been dreaming about—whether it's starting your own business, changing your career, or pursuing your passion—don't let the fear of risk stop you.

Calculate the risk. Prepare yourself. And then take the leap.

Because real success lies outside your comfort zone. And once you take that first step, you'll realize that *risk toh hai hi nahi.* It was just your mind creating imaginary fears.

<h1 style="text-align:center">Chapter 5</h1>

I AM LEARNING NEW THINGS (NOT JUST STRUGGLING)

Breaking Free from the Struggle Mindset

"Bas, main struggle kar raha hoon..."

How many times have you heard this phrase? Maybe you've even said it yourself. Whenever people start something new—whether it's launching a business, learning a skill, or stepping into a new industry—they often describe their experience as a **struggle**. It almost feels like struggle is the default mode when we aim for something big.

But have you ever stopped to think about what the word **"struggle"** really means?

The word itself feels heavy, doesn't it? It carries a burden, a sense of pain, exhaustion, and resistance. The more you tell yourself, *"I am struggling,"* the more your brain starts believing it. You feel stuck. You feel as if life is an uphill battle, and the weight of the challenge keeps getting heavier.

But what if you could shift your mindset?

What if, instead of saying, *"I'm struggling,"* you said, *"I'm learning"*?

Doesn't that feel different?

Struggle vs. Learning: A Shift in Perspective

When you reframe your experience as **learning** instead of **struggling**, something powerful happens.

Your mindset shifts from:

+ Feeling stuck → Feeling empowered

+ Carrying a burden → Embracing growth

+ Seeing problems → Seeking solutions

Because that's exactly what's happening—you are learning. Every challenge you face, every mistake you make, every setback you encounter—it's all part of your personal and professional growth.

+ Struggle drains energy. Learning fuels it.

+ Struggle feels like a burden. Learning feels like an opportunity.

+ Struggle leads to frustration. Learning leads to progress.

Would you rather feel trapped by struggle, or excited about learning?

The Journey vs. The Goal: Why the Process Matters More

One of the biggest mistakes people make is focusing entirely on the **goal** and forgetting about the **journey**.

They think, *"Once I reach my goal, I'll be happy. I'll be successful. I'll finally have what I want."*

But here's the reality:

The **journey** is everything. The **goal** is temporary.

Let's take an example.

Imagine you've set a goal to score **98%** in an important exam. You work hard, sacrificing sleep, weekends, and fun outings. You pour your heart into studying.

Finally, the results are out. You open your scorecard and see **97.6%**.

Now, how do you feel?

Some people might think, *"Bas, yeh toh failure hai. Maine 98% ka goal set kiya tha, aur yeh 97.6% hai. I failed."*

But is that really true?

If your happiness depends only on the **goal**, then yes, you might feel disappointed. But if you've enjoyed the **process**—the hard work, the knowledge gained, the discipline built—then you'll realize something deeper:

You didn't fail. You grew. You learned. And that is success.

Developing a Growth-Oriented Mindset

Mindset plays a crucial role in how we perceive success and failure.

Here's the truth:

Everything in life is temporary. **Success, failure, happiness, sadness—nothing lasts forever.**

And that's okay. That's what makes life exciting.

+ If you succeed, celebrate it—but don't stop improving.

+ If you fail, learn from it—but don't stop moving forward.

When you realize that success and failure are both temporary, you stop **fearing failure**. You stop **chasing after success** as if it's the only thing that matters. And you start focusing on what really matters—the **process, the learning, and the journey**.

The Real Meaning of Success

Most people define **success** as a **destination**, but in reality, success is about who you become along the way.

True success is not just about achieving a goal; it's about:

- The skills you develop
- The mindset you build
- The person you grow into

So, instead of obsessing over **results**, shift your focus to **enjoying the process**.

Because in the end, the **process** shapes you more than the **result** ever will.

Reframing Your Mindset: From Struggle to Learning

The next time you find yourself saying, *"Main struggle kar raha hoon,"* stop.

Instead, say:

"Main seekh raha hoon." (I am learning).

This simple change in language has the power to:

- Keep you motivated and positive
- Help you stay focused on progress
- Transform you from a victim to an **active learner**

Every experience, whether good or bad, is a lesson. And when you embrace **learning** over **struggling**, you begin to:

- ✦ Find solutions instead of excuses
- ✦ See opportunities instead of obstacles
- ✦ Feel excited instead of exhausted

The Temporary Nature of Success and Failure

Everything in life—success, failure, happiness, sadness—is **temporary**.

- ✦ Success? Celebrate it, but don't stop growing.
- ✦ Failure? Learn from it, but don't let it define you.

That's why it's so important to **stay balanced** and **keep learning**, no matter what happens.

Final Thought: Embrace Learning, Not Struggling

Life is not about **struggling**—it's about **learning, growing, and evolving**.

So, the next time you face a challenge, don't think of it as a **struggle**. Think of it as:

- ✦ A lesson
- ✦ A stepping stone

✦ An opportunity to become a better version of yourself

And always remember:

✦ Success and failure are temporary.

✦ But learning lasts forever.

Action Step for You:

The next time you feel like you're struggling, ask yourself:

✦ What am I learning from this experience?

✦ How is this challenge helping me grow?

Write down your answers. You'll be surprised at how much you're actually progressing.

Because at the end of the day... You're not struggling. **You're learning.**

Chapter 6

WHEN TO START OR TAKE A RISK

"Kab shuru karein? Kab risk lein?"

This is one of the most common questions people ask themselves. You have a dream, a passion, or an idea that excites you—but then your mind starts raising doubts.

"Kya yeh risk lena sahi hoga?"

"Abhi stable job hai, achha chal raha hai, weekend pe pub jaa sakte hain, trips kar sakte hain... Kya zarurat hai risk lene ki?"

"Agar fail ho gaya toh kya hoga?"

And suddenly, you stop. You delay. You hesitate.

Risk: Aisi Cheez Jo Hai Hi Nahin (It's All in the Mind)

Risk is one of the most misunderstood concepts. People think that risk is something dangerous, something to avoid at all costs. But in reality, *risk* is just uncertainty.

It's the fear of the unknown. And most of the time, this fear exists only in your mind.

Let's break this down.

Imagine you don't know how to swim. One day, you decide to jump into the deep end of a swimming pool. That's risky, right?

But what if, instead of jumping into the deep end, you start in the shallow end? You practice slowly, you learn how to float, how to paddle, and then gradually build your confidence. Now, is it still risky? No. Because you've calculated the risk, prepared for it, and taken small steps toward your goal.

Calculated Risk vs. Blind Risk

There are two types of risks:

1. **Blind Risk** – This is when you jump into something without any preparation, research, or planning. It's like driving a car blindfolded—you're bound to crash.

2. **Calculated Risk** – This is when you plan, prepare, and then take a well-thought-out risk. You assess your capabilities, gather information, and create a backup plan.

The key to success is taking **calculated risks**, not blind risks.

The Bike Overtaking Example

Think about when you overtake a car while riding a bike. You don't just accelerate blindly, right? You calculate how much speed you need, how far the other vehicle is, and whether you have enough time and space to overtake safely. That's a calculated risk.

The same principle applies to life. Whether you're starting a business, changing careers, or pursuing a dream, you need to calculate your risk and plan accordingly.

How to Plan Your Risk (Step by Step)

1. **Assess Your Risk Capacity:**

   Everyone's risk capacity is different. Some people can take big risks, while others prefer smaller, safer steps. Figure out what works for you.

2. **Do Your Research:**

   If you want to start a business, don't just quit your job overnight. Start by doing research on weekends. Study the market, learn the skills you need, and understand the challenges.

3. **Make Financial Plans:**

   One of the biggest reasons people fear risk is financial insecurity. So, plan your finances.

   ✦ Calculate your monthly expenses.

✦ Save enough money to cover at least 6 months of living expenses. For example, if your monthly expenses are ₹20,000, save ₹1,20,000 as a backup.

✦ Invest wisely and avoid unnecessary expenses.

4. **Surround Yourself with Ambitious People:**

Your environment plays a huge role in your mindset. Spend time with people who have big dreams, who take risks, and who inspire you to aim higher. Avoid negative people who discourage you or waste your time.

5. **Take Small Steps:**

You don't have to take a giant leap right away. Start small. Take one step at a time. Build your confidence gradually.

Enjoy the Journey, Not Just the Result

One of the biggest mistakes people make is focusing only on the result.

They think, *"Agar fail ho gaya toh log kya kahenge?"*.

But here's the truth: Success and failure don't matter as much as the journey.

When you take a risk, don't focus on whether you'll succeed or fail. Focus on enjoying the process. Learn from every experience. Even if you fail, you'll come out stronger, smarter, and more prepared for the next opportunity.

Why People Fear Failure

Most people fear taking risks because they're afraid of failure. They're worried about what others will say. *"Dekha, risk liya aur fail ho gaya."*

But here's a secret: **Failure is not the opposite of success—it's a part of success.**

Every successful person has failed at some point. The difference is that they didn't let failure stop them. They learned from it and kept moving forward.

The Key to Overcoming Fear: Change Your Definition of Failure

If you define failure as "not achieving your goal," you'll always be afraid of it. But if you define failure as "not trying at all," you'll start seeing things differently.

The real failure is not taking the risk. The real failure is staying in your comfort zone and never pursuing your dreams.

Final Thought: When to Start? The Answer Is NOW.

There's never a "perfect" time to start. You'll never have all the answers, and you'll never feel 100% ready. But that's okay. The best time to start is *now*.

Take that first step. Plan your risk, prepare for it, and then take action.

Because the biggest risk in life is not taking any risk at all. And the biggest regret is looking back and wondering, *"What if I had tried?"*.

So, stop waiting. Stop hesitating. Stop overthinking.

Take that calculated risk. Start your journey. And enjoy every moment of it.

Chapter 7

HOW TO FIND YOUR OWN KAASH (NO REGRETS)

Life is a journey, not a destination. Yet, most people go through it without truly living, simply following a path that was laid out for them by society, parents, or circumstances. They chase security, money, or societal approval—only to reach a point where they look back and ask themselves:

"Is this really the life I wanted?"

If you never ask yourself this question, you are lucky. But if you have, then this chapter is for you.

If you don't figure out your true purpose—your Kaash—your time will pass, and in the end, all you'll be left with is regret.

- ✦ The regret of not chasing your dreams.
- ✦ The regret of not taking risks.
- ✦ The regret of living for others, but never for yourself.

If you don't want to be one of those people, start today. Ask yourself:

✦ Am I truly happy with what I'm doing?

✦ Does my work excite me, or am I just doing it for money?

✦ What would I do if I didn't have to worry about money?

If you don't know the answers yet, don't worry. This chapter will guide you toward finding your own Kaash and living a life without regrets.

Are You Struggling with Concentration? A Hidden Sign

If you constantly struggle with concentration, feel distracted, or don't feel excited about your work, this is a warning sign that you're not working for your Kaash.

This is not a disease. It's not laziness.

It simply means you are doing something that doesn't truly interest you.

Think about it:

✦ When you love something, do you need an alarm to wake up? No.

- ✦ When you watch your favorite movie, do you feel distracted? No.

- ✦ When you're deeply engaged in a hobby, do you feel tired? No.

That's the difference between living your Kaash and living a life of obligation.

If you can't focus on your work, take it as a message from your inner self. You are not on the right path.

What to do?

- ✦ Find what excites you.

- ✦ Change your job, business, or approach.

- ✦ Don't settle for something that drains your energy.

It doesn't matter what people think. This is your life, not theirs.

Stop making others happy at the cost of your own happiness.

Because in the end, you will be the one living with regret, not them.

The Bhagavad Gita's Lesson: Your Fight, Your Responsibility

The Bhagavad Gita teaches us one of the greatest lessons:

In the epic battle of Kurukshetra, Lord Krishna was there to guide Arjuna, but Arjuna still had to fight his own war.

- ✦ Krishna didn't pick up a weapon to fight for him.
- ✦ Krishna didn't do the battle on his behalf.
- ✦ He gave him wisdom, showed him the way, but the battle was Arjuna's alone.

What's the lesson?

The same applies to your dreams.

- ✦ No one will fight for your dreams.
- ✦ No one will work day and night to make your goals a reality.
- ✦ No one will take risks on your behalf.

That's your job. And only you can do it.

If you want to change your life, you have to wake up, stand up, and take action.

Stop waiting for a miracle and start creating your own magic.

Life is Full of Suspense – Live It Fully

Life is unpredictable. It's full of ups and downs, surprises and suspense. But that's what makes it exciting.

Yet, most people live like robots—following a predefined path, never questioning it.

Born → Study → Get a Job → Marry → Earn → Retire → Die

That's the default setting of life.

But who decided this for you?

- Why can't your life be different?
- Why can't you live on your own terms?
- Why can't you create your own path?

Because society never told you that you could.

No one asks children, "What do you love doing?"

They ask, "What job will you get?".

No one says, "Follow your dreams."

They say, "Choose a safe career."

But here's the truth:

- You are not here to live someone else's life.
- You are not here to follow someone else's rules.
- You are here to live your own Kaash.

Real-Life Story: MS Dhoni – A Man Who Chose His Dream Over Stability

MS Dhoni is a perfect example of someone who followed his Kaash—his true passion—despite all obstacles.

1. **Leaving a Stable Job for a Dream**

   Mahendra Singh Dhoni had a secure government job as a ticket collector at the Indian Railways.

   - **He worked long shifts at Kharagpur railway station.**

   - **He still trained every morning, played matches, and kept practicing.**

   - **His parents wanted stability, but he wanted to play cricket.**

   Most people would have said:

   "I have a government job, life is set. Why take the risk?"

   But Dhoni was different. He didn't want to live with a regretful Kaash (*If only I had tried!*).

2. **The Toughest Decision: Taking the Risk**

   One day, he made the toughest decision of his life – he left his railway job to pursue cricket full-time.

   This was a huge risk.

- **No guarantee of success**

- **No backup plan**

- **People laughed at him (*"Cricket se pet nahi bharta"*)**

But he didn't care. His love for cricket was stronger than his fear of failure.

3. **From Small-Town Boy to World Champion**

   - **2004: Dhoni made his India debut—got out for zero runs.**

   - **2005: Scored 148 against Pakistan— India had found a new hero.**

   - **2007: Became captain and won the T20 World Cup.**

   - **2011: Hit the historic winning six in the World Cup final.**

If he had stayed in his railway job, he might have retired with a pension, but he would never have been a legend.

Lesson?

Don't settle. Take risks. Live your Kaash.

Final Thought: Finding Your Purpose

You don't have to be the best in the world at something to be happy.

You just have to do something that makes you feel alive.

Your Kaash is unique to you.

So, take a deep breath. Ask yourself:

- ✦   What do I really want?
- ✦   What's my dream?
- ✦   If I had no fear, what would I do?

And then, go after it with everything you've got.

Because when you follow your Kaash, you won't need to worry about the result.

No more Kaash—live without regret.

Chapter 8

HOW TO EXECUTE YOUR KAASH

Now You Are Ready with Your Kaash

Starting a new journey is easy. But staying committed and executing it till the end? That's where most people fail.

At the beginning, your dream (Kaash) fills you with energy and excitement. You imagine how life will change, how success will feel, and how people will admire you. But then, reality strikes.

The first failure comes.

The first negative comment hits you.

The first moment of doubt creeps in.

And suddenly, your excitement starts fading. You overthink, question yourself, and wonder, "Did I make a mistake?" But here's the truth:

Everyone dreams. Few execute. Fewer persist.

The world is filled with unfinished dreams—ideas that never saw the light of day because people gave up too soon. If you want to turn your Kaash into reality, you need more than motivation. You need execution, discipline, and consistency.

The Reality Check: Why Most People Quit

Before you learn how to execute your dream, you must understand why most people fail. Here's what happens when someone starts something new:

Stage 1: Excitement (The Beginning) – You feel unstoppable. Your vision is clear. You wake up early, work hard, and feel motivated.

Stage 2: Doubt (The Challenge) – The real world pushes back. You face obstacles, slow progress, and criticism. Your excitement drops.

Stage 3: Distraction (The Trap) – You hear people say, "This won't work." You start procrastinating, looking for excuses, and thinking of other ideas instead of staying committed.

Stage 4: Giving Up (The End) – You convince yourself that quitting is the best option. You say, "Maybe this wasn't meant for me." And your dream dies.

Most people quit at Stage 3. If you want to succeed, you must break this cycle.

What is the difference between successful people and failures?

Successful people push through the challenges and never stop.

Step-by-Step Guide to Executing Your Kaash

Step 1: Write Your Goals Every Single Day

A goal that isn't written is just a wish. Every morning, take a notebook and write:

+ **Your Long-Term Goal (What is your ultimate dream?)**

+ **Your Short-Term Goal (What is today's target?)**

+ **Your 'Why' (Why do you want this?)**

This simple habit will keep your vision clear and remind you every day why you started.

Step 2: Wake Up Early & Train Your Mind

Morning is the most productive time – no distractions, no noise.

Your mind is fresh. You feel in control.

Start with:

✦ **Reading something motivational**

✦ **Writing your goals**

✦ **Planning your day**

✦ **A 30-minute workout**

If you can't control your morning, you can't control your life.

Step 3: Surround Yourself with the Right People

Your environment shapes your mindset. If you listen to negative people, you will doubt yourself.

✦ **Find people who uplift you**

✦ **Join growth communities**

✦ **Follow mentors**

✦ **Leave people who don't support your vision**

Step 4: Break Your Goal into Small Steps

Big goals feel heavy. Break them into:

✦ **Monthly targets**

✦ **Weekly tasks**

✦ **Daily steps**

Daily wins build momentum.

Step 5: Stop Seeking Approval from Others

Don't wait for someone to approve your dream. They might:

- Laugh
- Doubt you
- Discourage you

But remember:

You are building your dream, not theirs.

Ignore the noise. Focus on your path.

Step 6: Discipline Over Motivation

Motivation fades. Discipline stays.

Ask yourself:

- "What must I do today, no matter what?"
- "How can I move forward even on tough days?"

Discipline is:

- Showing up daily
- Ignoring excuses
- Trusting the process

Step 7: Read and Learn Continuously

Don't wait to know everything. Learn on the go.

- ✦ **Read daily**
- ✦ **Learn new skills**
- ✦ **Stay curious**

Elon Musk didn't know how to build rockets; he learned by reading and doing.

Knowledge + Action = Success

Step 8: Visualize Success Every Day

Train your brain to believe it's possible:

- ✦ **Close your eyes**
- ✦ **Picture your goal achieved**
- ✦ **Feel the emotion**

If you can see it, you can create it.

Step 9: Fail Fast, Learn Faster.

Failure isn't the opposite of success – it's part of the process.

When you fail:

- ✦ **Don't overthink**
- ✦ **Learn the lesson**
- ✦ **Adjust and try again**

Each failure is progress in disguise.

Step 10: The Secret to Success – Stay Consistent

Small actions, repeated daily, create magic.

People will one day admire your success but miss the:

- ✦ Sleepless nights
- ✦ Rejections
- ✦ Sacrifices

The world rewards consistency.

Bonus Insight: Practice Over Theory

Reading about how to swim won't teach you to swim. You need to jump into the water.

And the same goes for your Kaash.

You can read every book, watch every video, and listen to every podcast, but if you don't practice, you won't grow.

Theory gives direction. Practice brings transformation.

So stop just learning. Start applying.

Don't just dream. Do.

Mess up. Fall. Learn. Repeat.

That's how real execution happens.

That's how dreams come true.

Final Words: Start NOW, Stay UNSTOPPABLE

Your Kaash is waiting for you. No one else will do it for you.

Stop waiting. Start doing.

Stop planning. Start executing.

The question is simple:

Will you commit to it?

Yes or No?

Chapter 9

BALANCE YOUR KAASH WITH YOUR DAILY LIFE

When you start working toward your Kaash—your dream—you must learn to balance it with your daily life.

Most people struggle with this balance. They either:

1. Go all in on their dream but neglect their health, family, and responsibilities.

2. Get stuck in daily life and never take action on their dream.

But the truth is, you do not have to choose between the two. You can create a system where you work on your Kaash while managing your daily life effectively.

Small steps create big transformations. First, your actions shape your behavior. Then, behaviors turn into habits. And ultimately, your habits define your life.

To stay on track, follow these essential daily steps.

Daily Routine to Balance Your Kaash with Life

If you do not create structure, life will always feel chaotic. A strong morning routine and a clear plan will help you stay disciplined while making progress toward your goals.

Step 1: Wake Up Early and Hydrate

Start your day with discipline. Wake up early and drink a glass of lukewarm water to cleanse your system and refresh your mind. This simple habit boosts metabolism, improves focus, and prepares your body and mind for action.

Step 2: Practice Meditation

Spend five to ten minutes in silence, focusing on your breath. Meditation helps clear your mind, increase focus and creativity, and reduce stress and negativity.

Even the most successful people in the world—Steve Jobs, Oprah Winfrey, and Virat Kohli—use meditation to keep their minds sharp.

Step 3: Write and Visualize Your Goals

Every morning, write down your goals for the day. Then, close your eyes and visualize yourself achieving them.

Writing your goals increases the chance of achieving them by 42%, according to research. Visualization activates your brain to find ways to make your goals a reality and helps you stay motivated and focused.

Step 4: Exercise for Energy

Engage in light physical activity—stretching, yoga, or a short workout. A healthy body supports a productive mind. Even a fifteen-minute workout can boost your energy for the entire day.

Step 5: Plan Your Day

Take five to ten minutes to create a structured plan. Prioritize tasks that bring you closer to your dreams while balancing responsibilities.

A successful day is a planned day.

Start Small and Avoid Overthinking

One of the biggest reasons people fail to take action is overthinking.

Most people focus too much on the big picture and get overwhelmed. They think about how they will become successful, what will happen if they fail, or whether they are wasting their time.

But here is the truth: You do not need to see the entire path to take the first step.

Imagine you are walking at night with only a small flashlight. If you stop because you cannot see the whole road, you will never move forward. But if you take one step at a time, the path ahead gradually reveals itself.

Start small.

Focus on today.

Take one step forward.

Never Wait for All Green Lights

Many people delay taking action because they want everything to be perfect before they start. They wait for the right time, the right opportunity, or the perfect plan, but that moment never comes.

Imagine this:

You are sitting in your car, waiting for every traffic light in the city to turn green before you start driving. That would be impossible.

But that is exactly what happens when people say:

+ I will start my dream project when I have more time.

+ I will follow my passion when I have more money.

+ I will take the first step when I feel completely ready.

The reality is that moment will never arrive.

Success does not come from waiting; it comes from starting.

You do not need all green lights to move forward. Just start the engine, drive to the first signal, and take it one step at a time.

If you wait for the perfect conditions, you will stay stuck forever. Start with what you have, where you are, and adjust along the way.

Real-Life Story: The Wright Brothers – Flying Without Permission

One of the greatest examples of not waiting for all green lights is the story of Orville and Wilbur Wright, the pioneers of aviation.

In the early 1900s, everyone believed human flight was impossible. They did not have funding, government support, or a degree in aeronautical engineering.

But they did not wait.

They worked with limited resources in their bicycle shop.

They failed hundreds of times before their first successful flight.

They took small steps every day, making improvements after every test.

Finally, on December 17, 1903, they flew the first-ever airplane.

Imagine if they had waited for the right conditions or until they had all the knowledge, money, and approvals—they would have never invented the airplane.

Take action with what you have. The right time is now.

Final Thought: Balance, Action, and Growth

Balancing your Kaash with daily life is about discipline, consistency, and patience. You do not have to take giant leaps—just start with small steps and keep moving forward.

Key Takeaways

- Follow a daily routine to create structure in life.

- Stop overthinking and take small, consistent actions.

- Do not wait for all green lights—start with what you have.

- Believe in yourself and trust the journey.

When you follow your Kaash with balance, focus, and action, success is no longer a dream—it becomes your reality.

No more waiting. No more overthinking. Take action today.